RED KITE, BLUE SKY

POEMS

❧

Madeleine May Kunin

RED KITE, BLUE SKY

POEMS

GREEN WRITERS PRESS | Brattleboro, Vermont

Printed in the United States

10 9 8 7 6 5 4 3 2 1

Green Writers Press is a Vermont-based publisher whose mission is to spread a message of hope and renewal through the words and images we publish. Throughout we will adhere to our commitment to preserving and protecting the natural resources of the earth. To that end, a percentage of our proceeds will be donated to environmental and social justice activist groups. Green Writers Press gratefully acknowledges support from individual donors, friends, and readers to help support the environment and our publishing initiative.

GReen
wRITeRs
press

Giving Voice to Writers & Artists Who Will Make the World a Better Place

Green Writers Press | Brattleboro, Vermont
www.greenwriterspress.com

ISBN: 978-1-9505849-8-7

COVER PHOTO: KATE POND
www.vermontsculpture.com

To my grandchildren,

Will, David, Sara, Sam,
Jacob, Charlotte,
and Thomas

CONTENTS

∽

Blue Sky

I have time—a bushel full,
no, a truck load, a storage unit
full of time.
Still, I portion time out carefully,
almost like in the old days,
except, now I stretch my neck
and raise my head
and keep it there until it hurts,
to look at the blue sky.
Long ago before Coronavirus,
I looked at the sky for weather,
or at night, for stars.
The blue sky gave me answers,
by the hour.
I didn't even say thank you.
Yesterday I went for a walk
and gazed upward, expecting little.
I looked up at the blue sky.
The longer I looked, I saw more layers of blue.
The blue sky had depth,
a clean teacup of blue without a crack.
I could see through one blue,
to find another blue.
The longer I held my head up
blue became more blue,
until I continued my walk
and thanked the sky for being blue.

ONE

RED KITE

Red kite seeks blue sky
soaring higher and higher
flipping its tail in and out
half circles, crazy dips.
A runaway kite
pulled in against its will
fights back, before it falls.

Are You Old?

Are you old,
am I young?
Not really, No.
I don't want you to slide
into that other place
with a slit
down the middle
that leaves me alone
in my superiority.

ON THE EVE OF MY 77TH BIRTHDAY

(while feeling sick)

The number is not mine, I do not own it.
My mother did not achieve it,
nor my grandmother.
No one got to two sevens,
side by side, like two soldiers.
Someday, I'll yearn to
return to that number.
Now I wish for a clear head
and a light chest: normal.
Will I make it to the next year?
Written in the Book of Life?
John, the elder, is John the younger.
I am glad he is complete,
while I break into pieces.
I will myself together,
for tomorrow, and begin to attach
all the broken bits,
into a new whole.

TURNING EIGHTY-ONE

I don't have to do somersaults
to be happy, I tell myself.
I am eighty-one, I don't
have to display my agility.

Even if I get short of breath,
pushing and panting uphill—
my resume suffices.
It is complete.
Like an apple.

But my hunger increases
as I age--like an infant
greedy at the breast.
I want to suck and suck
until the last drop
dribbles out.

EIGHTY-FOUR YEARS

My birthday, big
as a stop sign
red, blazing.
The number blinks
and calls me
forward: *this is*
who you are.
I stop at the curb,
waiting for the
light to change,
to let me move on
like I always did
when I was forty-four
and green.

Birthday Eighty-Six

First it was eighty,
then eighty-five.
Toppling over to eighty-six;
ninety rising on the horizon.
I gave a speech yesterday.
I made them laugh—
They clapped the years away.
How old am I, really?
Hard of hearing, afraid of falling,
my knees speak to me when I
go upstairs or down.
I take my medicine,
little white pills and a green one,
every morning and again at night.
But I could suddenly
become like her—over there,
strapped to her wheelchair
waiting to be pushed.

BIRTHDAY NINETY

I have two friends who turned ninety this month.
They are going to the opera in New York City
staying with a sister in New Jersey
to celebrate their birthdays together.
So why am I anxious turning eighty-six,
staying here at home
where I can sleep in my own bed at night
nap in the afternoon
wait for the clock to strike, done.

Obituaries

I read the young ones first
curious why they died early and
pleased with my self for living longer.
Then I seek out the 1930's
close to my birth year 1933.
Almost all had a courageous battle with death
and were surrounded by a loving family.
Sometimes I want to join them
in their ease, their resting place.
So much space is given to the dead
the best part of the newspaper.
I read them all
before I take an afternoon nap.

BROKEN

Crash!
So many pieces run
across the kitchen floor
under the sink, into
the hallway, free
no longer fastened
in crystal form.
Raspberries, sherbet,
cake—it held them all
until it slid off
the top shelf
where I stacked
plates hurriedly,
not thinking gravity
would force it down.
I am sorry.
Forgive me,
Dear Aunt Berthe—
it was yours
and became mine.
I sweep up the pieces,
so many, how can
there be so many?
I lift one to the light.
A thick rim piece
with a fluted edge.
Can it be saved?
No, too small

to round the curve
of the broken dish.
All together now
into the paper bag.
Music slides out.
I scan the wooden floor
one sliver, too small for my fingers,
could pierce the sole of my foot,
and draw blood.

CHRYSALIS

You came out
born anew, like
yesterday, almost
not quite, but
good enough for me.
How did you tear your
way out from the chrysalis
scratching all that time.
scratching, scratching
until you caught a thread
that unraveled into sight
and sound until you slid
back to me, arms
outstretched
wavering in the air,
when the ground rose
up to meet us.

Church Abuse

"Church Hid Abuse Of 1,000 Children, Grand Jury Finds"

How is this horror different from all other horrors:
Bombs, shootings, fire, floods?
One thousand boys and girls
twisted out of their childhood shapes.
So many, how could there be so many?
I crave details.
Rape, torture, shame.
One strung up on the wall
hanging naked like Christ.
I want more.
I want to give each child his name
untangle him from the one thousand.
I turn the page of the newspaper
and wonder about corn for dinner.

CONTAGION

We breathe the same air, in
the same room, in
the same bed
you and I.
Tiny droplets of depression
float into my lungs when
we are in a state of
dangerous proximity.
I cannot suit myself
from head to foot, goggles,
booties and gloves
impermeable at the seams
to contagion.
If only I could reverse
the current
from me to you,
instead of you to me.
Then we could embrace again,
skin against skin.

I'm Not The One Who Lives Alone

I am not the only one who lives alone
Betty, Ann, Kathy, and Carol.
All of us shut off the light for one,
scrunch towards the middle of the bed,
aiming to occupy his place.

The cat

I don't know how she knows—
greets me at the door.
I say hello, shyly.
Her eyes listen carefully
and I swear she understands
the void she is supposed to fill.

Lilacs

The lilacs were patient all year
packaged into
small ziplock bags
that allowed them privacy
in preparation for spring exposure.
They waited, until ripeness
burst them open,
releasing their lungs and dangling
their colors in the warming air.
How did they know when it was time
to offer their scent?
How did they know when to shrivel
into brown kernels that keep their secrets
and emit nothing?

GETTING OUT OF BED
or "March is the month of longing"

It's hard to pull myself
out of my bed at seven,
or even eight
like I used to do.
Fatigue is the weight
that presses me down
with a fist.
I weigh 300 pounds, or more,
when my head turns
but does not lift
from its hollow on the pillow.
Only five minutes more
I plead to my scolding self,
and she capitulates.
Nine o'clock,
My God!
How could that be?
I'm sleeping my life away—
an hour lost forever.

NEW LEAVES BURY

New leaves bury
last year's dead
layer upon layer
of snug suffocation.
The old leaves
accept without a cry
their colorful shrouds
that fall merrily down.
Not knowing that my
sightless foot will crush them
and scatter them to pieces.

Next to Me at the Concert

When I take my seat at the concert,
you are sitting next to me.
Almost two years later.
The music runs through you
before it reaches me.
Amplified by your body.
Once again, we listen
and sit back together.

Suicide

We talked about suicide:
her father, my father.
I had known her slightly,
we had met at parties
discussing the weather
or who would win the election.
Not life and death.
She had read my book.
I wrote about my father,
silently, confined to the page,
not ready for discussion.
She unlocked me
and to my surprise I opened up.
She recalled John (my husband):
He listened to her, she said, *as few men do.*
He did not seem depressed.
I had to explain his dark place,
Loss of sight, sound and mobility.
He stopped eating and drinking.
I paused, and continued,
in a way it was a suicide.
My throat constricted. I swallowed
and changed the subject.

SWIMMING

I read my notes of last summer.
Swimming, slim and strong.
I did not know what next.
A good thing.
Heavy sky, thick water,
each of us on a rock
he seated in suffering
me, with my nail file
trying hard, so hard
to allow love
to smooth us together.

The Fall

The earth is a burial ground
of brown paper-thin leaves.
Carelessly left alone
not a sound underfoot.
No sign that I was here.
One small black hoof
print left bare of leaves.
A deer who knows what
I don't know.
Brooding oaks,
storm-scarred maples
ask for my sympathy.
They have lost so many.
I must move on
trampling on their dead.

WISE OLD WOMEN DYING

My wise old women are dying
Alice, and Sally, and others.
They were my foremothers
who pulled me forward
and dropped heaps of wisdom
into my lap.
They generously filled
my pockets with courage
which I had caught in the air.
And held fast
Whenever a storm lifted me
off of my feet,
they found solid ground
and placed me there.
I was always the younger one.

In their presence,
they, always the older one.
If only by three years or so.

Now that they are gone,
I am moved up front.
I am the one to go to,
dispenser of wisdom
ready or not.

A Nice Day

I walked past a workman splattered with paint,
holding up a ladder.
Nice day I said casually and paused,
But it's hot.
A beautiful day! he exclaimed,
putting down his brush.
I wish I had spoken like he did.

Almost Spring

Today an icy ribbon runs down the road.
I test it with my foot: it is hard.
The day before, water leaked into my boot,
between my toes.

Dark clouds fasten the sky
a blue eye looks out
a ray of sun escapes
and warms my face.

Autumn

I would like to know the secret
of the dull brown oak
made of leaves that hold on
to the black branches—
with a force I cannot fathom.
I watch them sway every which way
in gusts that follow one another
in circles.
I see one fall, but it is
only a leaf swept up
from the ground
and tossed as if
it were still alive.

Before Spring

I long for a shaft of warmth from the sun
to touch my back, and reach down to my toes.
It's been a bitter winter, everyone says.
Arriving early before I found my gloves,
and staying until I lost one, then two,
sharp winds sliced my cheeks
and burned my brow
with a film of ice.
Yesterday snow sealed the fields again,
white, to the edge of the road
where gray mounds sit crystallized
with black specs, sequined together,
surrounded by a fringe of water
that flows downhill
and freezes at the base.
I caution myself, *don't slip.*
I step high over the water,
the raise my feet
over a slab of ice.
I dread that I will crash
into a jumble of elbows and knees,
and break my leg, injure my arm,
imprison myself in a stiff cast.
I long for the water to run to the sea.
I long for the sky to unfasten the clouds
and I long for the clouds to wash blue.

BLUE

Campaigning in Youngstown Ohio, Fall, 2016

A blind house stares at me.
Windows boarded up.
Blue trim, a pretty color.
The front door
a deep green.
The porch swept clean.
Who lived here?
Someone who cared about
the shade of blue
and left no trash behind.
Where have they gone?
Did they have to leave overnight,
their belongings thrown out on the street,
after they received the knock on the door?
Or did they carefully pack what they had
with plenty of time and drive to Grandma's
who was eager to take them in?
Or, are they still on the move,
looking for work, looking for a house
with fewer belongings and no toys,
still searching for blue?
Somebody now mows the front lawn.
The neighbors must have insisted
that the weeds be kept down.

Bracelet

Youngstown, Ohio

"I can't vote. I'm wearing a bracelet."
I had to think for a moment before I got it.
The young black man with spiky jelled hair
was polite. Well spoken.
"I got out of jail yesterday and can only walk
from here to the store."
He told me more:
"I was in for assaulting a cop,
but he assaulted me first."
"Are you in school?" I ask.
"I graduated from high school last June".
What came over me?
Here on this street
standing in his driveway.
"Stay clean and go to college.
You can get financial aid."
I told him, carried away by
my urge to become his savior.

DIAPERS

Youngstown, Ohio

I ignored his missing upper teeth
when I spoke to him the first time.
He wanted to talk.
I was there to ask him to vote.
He assured me he was registered
and would.
I walked across the street
and knocked on the door
of another house on our list.
He appeared again.
"That's my house,
I'm checking on my little girl.
It's not easy to be a single father."
I nodded.
Then he asked, "Do you know anywhere
I could get free diapers?"
"Have you tried welfare?"
"They don't give them out."
I thought of the sleeping baby.
Did he say she was three?
I ignored my thought
that three was too old for diapers.
I imagined a baby in dirty diapers,
crying in her crib.
"Wait a minute," I said.
I went to my idling car,
opened my wallet

and took out two fives and a ten.
I went back and gave him the money.
"He's probably going to use it to buy drugs,"
my friend remarked when I told her the story.
"I don't care," I said.
"I believe him."

Caregiver Blues

It's more mood than muscle
that is hard to lift
from walker to wheel chair.
He cannot fall,
not now, not again.
We fell side by side,
he backward, landed on his rear.
I forward, just missed the wheels
and arms of the deadly walker.
My neck hurt.
angry with him for standing up
without holding on.
The walker between us,
I could not reach across
to grab his hands.
Falling, out of control,
gravity, pushing him down,
pushing me down.
I am more upset than he is,
Speechless, out of breath.
I want to cry, out of frustration,
out of pity for him,
pity for me.

CAT

My cat plumps herself on the straight arm of my sofa.
Feet tucked neatly under her coat, purring her song.
She invites me to smooth her,
to feel her pillow under my hand.
I'm not invited inside her thoughts.
She sits mute as a Buddha carved from stone.
Whoosh!
She streaks to the next room, as if on fire,
sees something I can't see; hears something I can't hear.
Composed again, even sedate, she claims proximity.
Sits where I sit, walks where I walk, climbs across my lap
and seats herself regally by my side.
She stares intelligently at me as if ready for a chat.
Her coin-round pupils are circled in gold.
She holds her gaze until I give up.
A yawn unclips her red mouth, her pointy tiger teeth.
A beast.
Her mouth closes, her head is lowered,
Ah, we are companions once again.
Good kitty, I say in my baby voice
and think I'm falling in love.
Until she paws herself on to the dining table
as if it were her place, to sit across from me.
Off! I yell. Nothing.
Down! I shout. Nothing.
She is like an Egyptian statue, buried with Tutankhamen.
Impatient, irritated, I exercise my two-handed superiority
and drag her down, pulling against her needle paws.

She finds a chair that fits her form and sleeps the day away.
She is a night creature, silent in her roaming, until,
Crash!
I startle.
What is it?
Tablecloth askew, candle sticks toppled, candles unhinged.
My sweet cat, having terrified herself, has zipped into oblivion.
Together again, we sit on the sofa,
her flank wedded to my thigh.
Her small chin lifted high, rests on my arm;
I feel her cool breath hover over my willing wrist.
You're such a good kitty, I purr.
Lying in bed at night, I wait for her usual visit.
She gives no hint of her stealthy approach
A quick paw lands on my chest and then another,
until four paws have stepped over my body.
She plants herself on the other side, and searches until
she finds a nest, between my twig legs.
She curls herself into a coiled rope, no beginning or end.
We share our bodily warmth, hers intermingled with mine,
searching for our separate sleep.
I dare not move.

COUSIN IRENE

I miss my cousin Irene,
who lived in Zurich,
where I was born.
Her mother and my mother
were sisters.
My father and her father
were brothers.
That made us double cousins.
As a child I wanted her to be my sister
but she was an adult when I was twelve.
As I grew older we became closer.
We had a common past.
She knew where our grandparents' graves
were located in the Jewish cemetery,
and took me there.
How would I find them now?
She remembered my father—
he had slapped her
for dangling my brother out a window.
I wonder, how high?
Irene's mother died in childbirth.
The family tragedy.
Only to be equaled
by my father's suicide.
She treasured a few pages
of her mother's diary,
a slender gift.

Her mother, Alice, was sad, she learned,
jealous of her beautiful older sister.
Some afternoons
we sorted through photographs.
My father and mother linking arms in the snow, laughing.
Her father and our grandfather were there, too.
What fun they had
before I was born.

Could It Be

It is not a familiar headache.
This one is hard hitting
my skull against a granite wall.
The pain pulsing like a living thing
a throbbing frog on the
right side of my brow
turning on and off,
like a weak flashlight.
The pain is a blunt instrument
boring into my brain.
Fearful words crawl into the
crevices of my mind
and take up a lot of space.

Could it be
a blood clot inching along
the elastic vein to my heart
where, upon arrival,
it will strike me dead?
Or could it be a tiny tumor,
declaring itself to my body
for the first time?

My mother had a brain tumor,
that killed her.
I bury the back of my head in my pillow
and look out the window.
It is a nice day.

I Could Shoot Myself

I could shoot myself.
No, no don't say that.
I don't know how to go on
I can't think straight.

Oh yes you can, we're going
to the meeting, you'll see
it will be fine.

I stared at his plate, a ham
sandwich. I don't eat ham.

Take a bite I coaxed.
Please, eat it or
we'll be late.
We're going, now!

He rubbed his forehead
with his right hand, wiping it clean.
I wheeled him there, to the table
Up close, where they all sat.
I picked him up an hour later.
He smiled, at everyone
and laughed at a secret joke.
I could have killed him.

I Knew I Was Loved

When you were alive
I knew I was loved,
like a child knows her mother.
My words floated in the air
and landed on your fingertips
before you flicked them back to me.
How free I felt, coupled at your side.
The sinews of memory are strong;
stretching me back to where we walked,
when your steps paced with mine.
My shoulder weighed by your hand.
We saw the same sights.
Our thoughts were twins.
Now that you are gone,
I know I was loved
and that is (almost) enough.

SUNNING MYSELF

I was sitting by the lake
pulling myself away from the world
working hard on withdrawal,
gazing down at the stones below
and up at the slow moving sky
when my escape was blocked by
the news of the day.
Two mass shootings, nine dead in Dayton
twenty more in El Paso.
Many more wounded.
Interviews with bystanders
who had nothing new to say.
Still, I kept the TV on,
wanting more.
The camera moved to a woman who wept
into a large man's shoulder.
To a girl who carried a white sign with pink lettering:
Free Hugs.
She did what she could, poor thing.
A reporter, hungry for footage,
held the microphone to someone's twisted face,
doing her best to be kind.
To think, that all this time when it happened.
I had been busy sunning myself.

ONE YEAR LATER

It's been a year since you died.
I feel better, now, in some ways.
Shovelful, by shovelful
I filled you in,
level with the earth
that contained mounds of memories.
Sailing up the Nile I remember
seeing a farmer on the shore
and ancient ruins behind him
still standing there for us.
I remember
walking around Mount Saint Victoire
inhaling lavender
while slipping on small yellow rocks.
I remember
opening the balcony door
of our fourth-floor Paris hotel
and looking at blossoming trees below.
I remember
walking to the top of the street
and discovering the Arc de Triumph.
So close.
I remember the sweet sound of bells
as sheep scampered down
a path next to our hotel,
somewhere in the Lake District.
One year later, I turn the pages
of my photo album
and find you.

PLUM-COLORED GLOVES

My daughter gave me plum-colored
leather gloves a year ago.
Made in Hungary.
Baby soft.
I bring them together,
palm against palm.
I place one bare hand
over the gloved other.
Slip covered bone
stretched taut.
They've been in a box
for almost a year,
for safety.

Gloves are easy to lose,
they fall out of pockets,
abandoning their mates.
I've held on to widowed gloves
too long, hoping for coupling.

Now, at eighty-three
I take my new gloves out
and pull them on, like new skin.

SCARRED

I am scarred.
Two red stripes scratched
like railroad tracks
above my breast.
The cat did it.
The beast exploded
and chiseled my skin
while I sat reading on the couch
in my white night gown
top button left open.
She had climbed over me before,
carefully, claws withdrawn
as if I were her pillow.
I liked her purposeful paws,
stepping on me, one by one.
What mistakes had I made tonight
to unleash her terror
and tattoo her mark on me?
Not her fault, I tell myself,
staring into her wicked yellow eyes.

Stay Put

Stay put, where I know the steps,
how high the curb
how deep the cracks
how narrow the view
how safe I am on familiar ground.
I want to open the window wide
and breath new air
for the wider view
of unfamiliar ground.
Where I can see
a one-hundred year old olive tree,
hear a language I don't understand,
taste bitter and sweet on my tongue
and become a stranger in a distant land.
Before I trace my way back
to the soil I have known,
spread evenly
under my feet,

THE CANE

Where is your cane, in which arm?
I position myself to take the other.
Quickly, before you sink into
a sudden sway and disaster.
Linking arms we could be
mistaken for lovers, but
not with my eyes focused
on your seeking feet.
I'd rather we held hands
like lovers, our eyes
open to each other,
than have you grasp
my upper arm too tightly
like a banister, wooden,
tacked against the wall.
I walk without complaint.
Except to say,
hold on, hold on.
I try to match your pace
and strain not to walk faster.

THE FALL

John says *Let's do it* to my question:
a lecture, dinner, a walk,
he's ready.
He's almost new again
with hardly a bruise.
I watch him
steer his red walker
down the sidewalk.
I caution against cracks
and swollen bumps
to keep him from the edge
where the sidewalk meets
the grass, unkindly.
Uneven and suddenly,
the fall.
I won't do that again. He says,
picking himself up.
No harm done,
not this time.

Understanding Beethoven

I look at the stars and do not know all the constellations,
except for the Big Dipper.
I listen to music and do not know all the composers.
Except for Mozart.
I hear a lecture on Beethoven
and wish I had heard it long ago.
My knowledge is as thin as a sheet of waxed paper.
Facts are dead on the beach, so many washed away.
I want my knowledge to be laid out neatly
set down in its proper place, easily reprieved,
leaving room for fresh facts to find me.
So many layers to dig through
with my rusty spade before
I find what I want.
I want details.
How did Beethoven compose when he was deaf?
and write down notes for us?
I want to see Picasso at work,
Rembrandt in his dress-up clothes,
Rodin molding clay
chipping stone,
Bach at the organ in church.
I want to know music, art, astronomy, philosophy—
let it all come to me quickly
let me understand how the world was made.
Now, before I die.

WE

I liked being "we."
We were doubles,
not one, but two.
Walking in tandem.
When I was silent,
You spoke.
When I spoke,
You listened.
I drank your words
as if they belonged to me.
We fed on each other's
out pourings
before we whisked them together
into *"we," "us,"* and *"ours."*
"We" is a habit you
left me with.
So comfortable
and strong.
"I" is skinny.
It stands alone
brittle to the touch.
It needs something
at its side.
"I"
"I am"
"I am alive."

WEATHER REPORT

The weather report keeps me alive.
I must know the temperature,
cloudy or sunny,
hot or cold,
unusually warm for this time of year.
Or high winds anticipated.
Curiosity tingles me awake.
The weather saves me
from frozen sleep
until I thaw
in the warm light
and unwind myself
from my curled-up pose—
drop my gown,
free my wrists—
listen to the weather report
tell me what to expect
on this new day.

The Wheelchair

Damn, damn, damn.
Strong language for a man who doesn't curse.
He releases his venom
at the wheelchair.
He moves when I move
his white bald head
in front of me.
A platform for a kiss
so inviting
for my lips.
He pedals his feet
down the hall
as far as he can go.
A grown man
seated while
all are standing.
A child
among grown-ups
trying to be heard
from below.
Trying to be seen
from above,
before someone trips on a wheel,
and says, "Excuse me,
I'm sorry."

When I Was Sick

When I was sick with stinging cramps
and I could not carry my eyelids open,
every morsel felt sticky in my mouth
and my stomach chewed out loud,
I promised, to whom, to God?
That was when I returned to the land of the well.
I would take a deep breath,
deeper than everyday breath,
and exhale like a bellows.
I would thank God, or someone
very much like her,
for being alive a while longer.
I would look at the lake until I was bored,
I would find where the sky and the sea fit together.
I would be content,
by doing nothing, nothing except breathing.
And being grateful.

Baby Thomas, Big Sister

When Sam and Jacob were born
I prayed I would live until their Bar mitzvahs.
My wish was granted last Saturday
in the old synagogue
where Jacob recited his portion of the Torah, flawlessly.
Today baby Thomas is seven days old.
I lean into his bassinette—
where Edgar and I once slept—
and hover over his form
fresh from the womb,
his eyes fluttering now and then,
his face half hidden by his blue woolen cap,
to keep his body heat safely inside.
I count thirteen years, until his Bar Mitzvah.
I will be far away when
he sings his Torah portion.
But I know him now,
the new little man
wrapped in the blanket
I knitted for him stitch-by-stitch.
His two-year-old sister, Charlotte,
thrown over daddy's shoulder
like a sack of potatoes,
shrieks with delicious terror,
knowing Daddy is safe
Mommy is safe,
and she is the big sister.

Words

Words, my darlings, don't leave me.
I reach for you in the void,
White with emptiness.
Fingers curved
I clutch at vapor
And feel nothing.
I turn to the alphabet
A, B, C, D, E, G.
Like the child I was,
playing hide and seek:
Come out, come out
Wherever you are.
Oh!
My ghost word
jumps out from behind the tree,
incised in the black trunk,
raw to the veined touch
of my trembling hand.

Writer's Block

I turn my face into the pillow
to find that soft spot
that lets me breath darkness.
Morning, my lids open like a rose
and tell me it's
time for doing.
I must not join the cat in her sunken repose.
I have to shower, dress,
empty the dishwasher;
put everything away,
and make the bed.
I reach for words
that run from me,
I chase them around the corner
until they stumble
and I can write them down.

THE BED

These were my sheets and his bed.
These are not the right sheets. He said,
letting the corner limp down over the edge.
Just tuck them in. I said, with a hint of annoyance
that he didn't know better.
They always fit on my bed.
I said exactly what I thought,
knowing that I might
not be understood, or worse, offend.
There was a slight grating echo in our words
which we heard in different ways.
In other times, with other people,
it would have shredded the tie that bound them,
but in this time, with the two of us,
the tear was so quickly rewoven,
that we looked at each other
and laughed.

Can There Be More to Say?

Can there be more to say after
we have said everything there
is to say about oatmeal, warm toast,
and sliced bananas?
The weather has words.
I find them and report
that I wear gloves
but no boots, not yet.
He is inside and I am out
where the air is colder
than it was yesterday.
Chances of snow
mixed with rain.
One never knows
which way it will come down.
We have no plans that
have to be changed.
We talk about dinner:
what time, what place,
dining room or café?
Small morsels of words fill
us up until we pause,
take a breath, and devour
another sentence.

I Loved You When You Did The Dishes

I cooked, you did the dishes.
Did I love you for that?
I listened to the distant
clattering in the kitchen
while I sat in my chair,
reading the newspaper.
We shared most tasks then,
but you did the driving
and I could sit
still by your side,
with only a rare glance in
the rearview mirror to
check if it was safe to pass.
Now I do everything:
cook and wash the pots
and meet
the dishwasher's
greedy demands.
I make the bed, which you once
made when we slept together.
I push your wheelchair,
and straighten my back,
not letting it sink
into a stoop
before its time.
I feel my muscles tighten,
up the incline;
I wish you could feel it, too,
from your glued position.

You need me now to move
in any direction:
up and down,
and around corners,
without bumping into
things, like winter boots,
thrown casually on the floor.
I take the lead, pulling
you out of yourself, and into
the world I inhabit.
You visit me, from time to time,
like you used to do
when you did the dishes,
and the counters always
needed wiping.
This evening is better than
this morning, when you berated yourself
for growing old.
"What can I do?" you asked,
pleading with yourself.
I whispered, "Nothing."
Evenings we meet on the sofa
and talk about a story in the New York Times.
Or a scene from the evening news.
We are same-minded again;
the world is spinning
crazily, out of its orbit.
We shake our heads
from side to side
in rhythmic disbelief.
I reach for your still hand,
cover it with mine,
and keep it there.

Hands

The woman sitting next to me
has purple-veined hands,
thick as ropes.
I look at my hands,
only a shade lighter.
Inky veins bulging
out of my paper skin.
How could I be
almost like her?

December 21, 2016

I made my bed this morning,
wanting to get back in.
The white duvet won't
stay flat like it should
at seven in the morning.
Puffiness beckons
me to lie supine
as white light
sinks me into sinful
repose, devoid
of dreams
and things to do
and places to be
on the dot of time.
Why not live back to front
and enjoy the best part
of the closing day in the morning.
When lavender drops
fall on my pillow,
and my feet find heat
at the foot of the bed.
I prop my head
and coax the light to
my open book, I want
so much to finish,
before I disappear.
from myself.
I would have to be sick

or dead
to get permission
to smooth the covers
sweetly over my body
in daylight.
I dare not ask,
not yet, not yet.

I Am Multiples

The dancer's
elastic poses
stretch my legs
high and wide
air up, I fall
on his raised hand
as if nothing
had happened.
The opera singer sways
my sucking ribs.
Her high octaves
tremble my bones
and wrinkle my throat
as I spill
gallons of sound
all over myself.
I'm on the tennis court
with someone else's arm,
Venus or Serena?
My body obeys
every quick command
from head to foot.
Look.
Just inside the line
by half an inch,
the camera assents.
The cello is settled between
bent legs, and curved arms

leaving fingers free to run
up and down, in
pursuit of fleeing notes
that I gulp down
into a thick, low sound
that feels good inside.
I abscond with the poet's words
and claim them for my own.
Or were they mine,
in the beginning?
I mouth them
with tongue and teeth,
and spit them in your face.
The writer says what I
wish to say,
leading me from
room to room in her house,
which seems eerily familiar.
She lived there once.
Chisel, brush, pen
bare faced, fully awake
ready for action.
Move, they say, like
we did, and make a mark.
I do, asking Monet, Manet
and ninety-year-old Picasso
to leave me a space.
I am multiples
and I am none.
It is late,
it is done.

Teeth

I spit them out like olive pits,
tainted yellow and hard,
uprooted from the cave
of my cheek, where my
tongue fingers empty rooms.
I contort my smile
to hide the hag
I have become.
My tongue takes
measurements
in and out,
back and forth.
My lids seek light
I open wide,
one tooth hanging
on the edge of a cliff,
another set in a tub of space
where it may wobble
and loose balance.
I panic at the thought.
I must bare my teeth
in self-defense.
I must chomp my way
into old age.
Ah, I smile
and open wide
and lift my electric toothbrush
off of its solid base,
and brush and brush
and brush.

ANTS

I spared a spider her death
in the bathtub this morning.
She was doing no harm.
Let her live.
I get kinder as I get older,
more forgiving.
I step into the kitchen,
black ants crawling on the counter,
ants upside down on the walls.
My hand sweeps them to the floor,
quickly, not thinking,
I stomp on them
one by one by one.

Christmas Cookies

Swiss Christmas cookies,
you remembered
making them in our kitchen.
Why should that make me so happy?
Zimmet Sterne, Basler Leckerli,
Spitzbüben with raspberry jam.
You wanted to make some
with your brother in his kitchen.
My recipes were hard to read
smudged by bits of butter,
fingerprints of flour.
We went to the Internet and
found almost what we wanted.
The first batch failed because you
mistook powdered sugar for flour.
No wonder!
You turned red with laughter.
The next batch was perfect:
six-pointed stars with slivered
almonds on top.
You thought they should have been
darker, as you remembered.
But they were beautiful
and tasted just right.
I had been a good mother,
after all.

PLANETS

Seven new planets
circling a star
named Trappist-1,
forty light-years
from our earth.
Swirling globules
all in a row,
there may be water;
there may be life.
I am entranced,
curious like
a wide-eyed child:
another earth,
another life,
I will not know.
I will not live
long enough.
I will not know
my newborn granddaughter
when she falls in love.

New Year's Eve at Wake Robin*

The wheelchair danced in circles
to the rapid beat of the
Onion River Jazz Band.
She was young again,
unbound, free,
no longer pushing him,
but flying with him
on the dance floor.
He waved aside the
ribboned oxygen tube
streaming behind him.
I grasped John with both hands
And brought him to his feet,
placing the walker within reach.
He moved his head, and then his arms,
and then his feet to the music.
We danced, we sang,
with the walker between us,
and love inside us.

*Wake Robin is a continuing care community.

A Love Poem

Each night
I wheel you to your door
with a kiss on your lips.
I smile my love at you,
generously, I think.
You don't know how much I love
you, you say.
I do, I do.
We've formed a ritual
of waving goodbye as I retreat
slowly down the hall.
At first, I wave with one
hand in the air, and then
my arms go wild before
I turn the corner,
as if struck by a storm
or signaling for help.
We wave in tandem.
You are there, and I
am here.
The nurses now know
we wave not for them,
but for one another;
to have and to hold
the love we swore to
once and forever.

TWO

COVID-19

Isolation

My feelings are hurt when my cat doesn't come up to my bed when I am ready to go to sleep. Doesn't she love me at night as much as during the day when she wedges herself between my thigh and my sofa, waiting to be stroked? When I am almost asleep I feel her four paws pressing down on my shoulder and indenting my stomach. It feels good. I am happy to feel her intrusion. Should I turn to my left side or my right? Asking the cat for permission. Because, and this sounds so silly. She is saving my life.

HOARDING

The clerk at the hardware store
met me in the parking lot, curb side.
Bird seed, he brought it out,
a shopping cart full
of fat bags leaning over the side.
I was embarrassed.
I had ordered three, twenty-five pound bags
Without knowing how big they were
or how heavy. I couldn't lift them
either into or out of the trunk.
Helpless, I asked the healthy looking young man,
can I exchange them for five or ten pound bags, please?
He obliged, unaware that he was risking his life
for the birds. So was I.
I could not, would not, run out of birdseed.

My Day

I wake up to a new day, but it is the old day
repeating itself.
I bend down to pee, stand up to brush my teeth and
    splash my face awake,
first my eyes and then my mouth, pulling away the crusts
    that adhered in the night.
Time washes downhill, without interruption,
except for meals which I force into a time slot
in order to pretend to be normal,
breakfast, lunch and dinner.
Sometimes I slip up---breakfast slides into lunch and
I eat dinner any time—
It does not matter, either before or after the news.
Having done nothing I can talk about, I look in the mirror
    and am dead tired.
My body yearns for my bed, a few feet away.
Fresh sheets yesterday. Proud of my work.
What would happen, I ask between yawns, if I went
    straight to bed,
skipped all those night t time obligations, so tiresome so
    tiring?
Would my mouth turn rancid in the night, and my eyes
    stay shut in the morning?
After all, these are not ordinary times. Nothing is as it
    was.
Why not delete the lovely word: ablutions
and submit to sleep? Pause.
I am almost seduced into sin, by the thought.
But not quite.

A Milestone

I am advised not to watch too much television.
It's bad for my mental health.
They are right.
But I watched the governor announce
seven hundred and seventy nine deaths yesterday
in New York alone.
Every number is a face, the governor said
and every face is a family.
I force myself to visualize these numbers
and pause long enough to mourn them,
to allow sadness to blossom freely
out of respect,
out of fear that my death
when it finds me, will be another number,
even a milestone.

Zoom Seder

First I saw my face appear on the computer screen
puffier than I imagined.
Then my daughter holding her six-month-old nephew, smiling
It was his first Seder.
I cooed...
Others popped up, almost from nowhere,
two grandchildren standing
at a dining room table with their blurred parents behind them
another pair of husband wife perched side-by-side on a sofa
like ghosts turned solid
before they were snuffed out by Zoom.
It was a miracle.
The thread of tradition, frayed in places,
was rewoven by long stretched wires.
The Egyptians would have been dumbstruck
the Jews have survived.
Arthur, who used to be my husband,
took his role as Leader seriously
finding a robust voice.
I asked, where did he find that sound
at the age of ninety-four?
I heard a jumble of voices
speaking at once because
we could not see who should go
next in the prescribed order of things.
We canceled each other out.
According to an invisible signal,

we fell silent, paused, and waited
for the next voice to jump out
to bless the matzo, the parsley dipped in saltwater,
the bitter and the sweet.
There was no meal we could share together,
matzoh ball soup, gefilte fish, and brisket.
Each family retreated to its own dining room table
sensing the void and wanting to remain together.
We skipped to the last pages of the Haggadah
and allowed our voices to be liberated and loud.
"ONE KID, ONE KID WHICH MY FATHER BOUGHT
   FOR TWO ZUZEEM"
from beginning to end.
Tradition, tradition
the story of Passover had been recited once again.
We had kept the pandemic hidden, if only for one night.

LOCKDOWN

Lockdown, is a criminal word,
What is the crime?
There is no concertina wire,
Concertina (a musical word)
to keep me within the circumference.
Circumference (a many syllabled word).
Yet I feel the invisible fence vibrating
the kind that shocks dogs
to keep them within bounds.
There were endless days, before the plague,
when I didn't want to leap out of bounds.
I didn't feel the pull of the leash.
But now that the fence encircles me
I want to get pliers.

Thinking of Death

At eighty-six, I think of death.
Not all the time,
but more often than before
the pandemic exploded
and covered me with ashes
sweeping the sky dark.
I find myself in a box,
chalk-marked *old,*
least likely to win the competition.
I have fallen into this slot
innocently, stacking up years.
An accomplishment of sorts;
I have lived a good life,
my death, will not be tragic.
It is too late for that.
I believe the old should go first.
Given a choice, the young must be saved.
It is perfectly natural.
Except when I feel the claws of the pandemic
wreathe my neck
and stifle my breath.

Home Alone

I think too much about myself
when I am home alone.
No one reminds me to get up at eight
or turn off the light at eleven.
I sleep past the alarm, and feel remorse
for lost minutes, even hours.
I used to be punctual, arriving in good time
for dentists, doctors, and friends.
The hands of the clock held me fast,
marked my movements around the day.
The pandemic has sickened my clock.
It can no longer tell me what day it is.
I luxuriate in being timeless, living alone,
except when I open my eyes
to my jittery television screen
and the head of a fully gowned nurse appears
who tells me she has just finished her ten-hour shift,
and is going back to work.

Beautiful COVID-19

The photo of COVID-19 greets me on the news every night.
It is brilliant,
pretty red clusters, the color of geraniums
dance in a framed circle.
If the virus were a flower, I would pluck it,
and put it into a clear glass vase
to admire on the mantelpiece.
A beautiful virus, lethal to the touch.
Every petal spits out venom
that can scar the branches of my lungs
steal my breath and walk away triumphant.

WELTSCHMERZ

Weltschmerz
is the right word for the weight
that presses down on me
and rounds my shoulders
in this time of pandemic.
Weltschmerz is a German word,
the first language I spoke
with a Swiss dialect.
It is hard to translate.
I break it in half and get
two words: "world" and "pain."
They cleave together
 in a noxious fog
that stings my eyes
and brings on tears.
Such a worldly pain is different from other pain
that I can trace back to myself.
Weltschmerz is an encircling sorrow
felt for the suffering of the world.
It is opaque. It is heavy,
too heavy, by far, to lift alone.

The Handshake

My right arm used to jut out like a jack in the box
to reach for a stranger's hand
when I was marching on the campaign trail,
in the old days, before the coronavirus.
Pressing the flesh, it was called then,
an expression I rejected.
I was certain that each handshake had meaning.
My hand was sending a message:
"This is who I am, trust me."
A stranger, who was caught by my hand,
had to respond to be freed
with a firm grip or a weak one,
rough or smooth?
When a gargantuan hand
incised my wedding band into my finger,
I cried, "Ouch!"
Was that my punishment or his mistake?
I stretched my grimace into a smile
and had to forgive him.
Not all handshakes were firm,
some hands were suspended in the air
limp as a tip toed ballerina
waiting to be caught by her partner.
Now, standing six feet apart,
further than two arms can reach
We keep our hands dutifully by our sides.

EARRINGS

I put my earrings on most mornings
during this eyeless pandemic
that doesn't see whether I'm wearing
silver hoops or tear-drop pearls.
Some mornings I get impatient
with my earring exercise,
when I can't find
the hole in my earlobe
to plunge my little dagger through.
When I miss my target,
a pin-point of blood
ekes out; a prelude to infection?
I worry.
Are the openings in my ears shutting,
not wanting to work anymore?
They know I am the only one to see them.
I look in the mirror
to make sure that one earring
hasn't dropped off.
I can't be lop-sided.
Not now.
With two earrings hinged in place.
I must appear balanced.

"I Can't Breathe"

I am falling into fear
unwinding
The ties that bind
Are splitting
Into shreds that float
from a virus infested sky.

A black man couldn't breathe
Because a white man
Pressed down on his neck
'Mama,' he cried, before
He died after almost nine slow minutes.

I sit in my chair here at home
Where I try to move close
To where they march down
pulsating streets
Opening their red mouths
to needle pointed smoke
Choking on injustice

THREE

SICILY

White Pillows

My mind is a clean white shell
as white as the inside of my wrist.
I sit in the sun, on white square pillows
Almost dry from last night's rain,
or did it pour this morning, while I slept?
The sea and the sky cover my mind's canvas,
leaving room for footloose clouds.
I tilt my hat to defend against the Sicilian sun
The skin around my ankles is sock covered.
I am satisfied with my caution, an old woman letting go
Having cast off things to do, now, later, never.

SELINUNTE

Columns, spaced against the blue sky, still standing
since five hundred years before Christ
a vestige of who they were, bowed to a God
we do not know.
Built by a slave we cannot pity,
tumbled by an enemy we do not fear.
I climb steps carefully one at a time,
Up is easy, down I hold your hand
fearing the fall that could force me
to join them in their layered graves
sealed with golden flowers, growing
since that first stone
was raised above another.
Their offspring have bedded themselves
into sun fed brilliance, gold against dry stone.
Columns alive in their height, refusing to fall.

SICILIAN SUN

The Sicilian sun melts
my argument against myself,
heat coating my body with forgiving warmth
that pierces my bones.
I search for who I am,
who I may become
before death drags me deep.

My eyes browse the surface
of the sea and the sky
I have loved, but not long enough.
I have wept when love left me.
I rest on the line
where the sea drops from the sky.
I slip into the water
deep, cold and black.

I flail against the wall,
gulp against my will.
fight against the pull.
Thrust up again
I sputter for breath
blink at the light.
Reach for the sun
and breathe.

Sciacca Poterie

I buy a bowl big enough for olive pits
Nothing else.
Slender blue fish swimming inside
To remind me of a place I hardly know
But want to remember that I have been.
Short old men sunning themselves,
three and four together.
Grandmothers holding miniature people by the hand,
dressed nicely.
I teeter on a disappearing strand of sidewalk.
Cars, too dangerous to trust, yet I do.
believing they are not interested in my death.

SEA BREATH

The sound of the sea
follows my breath
carried by the wind,
without pause, one long
glide stumbling into the next.
Turning, falling coming up
for air. Without end.
Blue turning green,
Green turning gray.
Not enough words
to mimic
the nervous sea,
fastened with bits of lace
lifting up here and there,
before being pulled down again.
The sea breaths in and out
endlessly sucking and spewing
long after my breath is spent.

FOUR

No Longer

No longer will we make love
before breakfast.
No longer will I dream
of seeing New Zealand
or the Cape of Good Hope.
Or bears in the wild.
No longer will I say
"Yes" more than "No."
No longer will danger sparkle
and safety look dull.
No longer will I look
at my body
without comparison
between who I was,
and who I have become,
blaming the light for
the difference.
No longer can I toss my hair
over my face,
and count one hundred strokes.
No longer can I do without
Night Cream and Day Cream,
slathering on, ounce after ounce.
No longer can I be comfortable
sitting in my chair, reading for hours
without getting up
to stretch my arms and legs.
No longer can I walk without

looking down at my feet
to avoid mean cracks and
malicious bumps.
No longer can I skip down
stairs like a girl, flying,
without feeling a thing.
No longer can I approach
the precipice without
swaying against my will.
No longer do I think ahead
of where I will be in ten years,
or twenty or more;
now I think in ones or twos or threes,
long enough to still hunger
for the food of life.
No longer do I wish for
the next day, or the next year,
to come quickly,
like I did the year
I turned ten.
I want the days to saunter,
like a leisurely
museum stroller who stops
now and then to gaze;
and get closer to the canvas
to see the brush strokes,
and then steps back
for the long view,
before moving on.

Voyage

Last night,
I thought about my mother's
voyage to America: what she faced
by herself, saying goodbye to all the relatives,
at the Zurich train station, accepting
prettily wrapped boxes of chocolate
from everyone,
and given to me
on the train
to carry safely
in a sack, heavy for a
six year old.
Left behind on the train;
how awful.
Did my brother make it up?
Or did this happen: that Nazi
soldiers walked through the train
questioning everyone?
The conductor vouched for my mother
having met her regularly
on the commuter train in Zurich.
I remember how scratchy the blanket was
in the sleeping car—that's all.
Waiting in Genoa for our boat to arrive,
our names on the manifest, with
an H for Hebrew, I found out later.
I looked out the window from the top floor
Of the hotel and saw—we thought—

Japanese soldiers lined up in formation,
ten days before Italy entered the war.
My mother did not unclothe her fear to us.
We found our cabin, already occupied,
by two women and a baby.
We settled in, somehow,
lugging the big blue trunk,
(which stood upright
and opened sideways).
Safely inside our cabin on the SS Manhattan,
I was delighted by the new taste
of apple pie à la mode,
and playing shuffle board on the tilting ship.
We lined up alphabetically at the pier
under the letter "M" for May
with a couple named Muller,
who became our friends and
gave each of us a beautiful
book every Christmas.
Finally, cousins Fred and Irene Kahn
found us.
She, already American,
Wearing a red hat, red shoes, red pocket book
opened our eyes wide:
"Mudlin, you have to have coils,
all the goils in Amerika have coils."
We repeated her words for years,
silly with laughter.

ABOUT THE AUTHOR

I couldn't write poetry when I was caught in the tempo of politics—as governor, as a federal official, and as an ambassador. My schedule was broken into twenty minute squares. As I eased into private life, a new door opened. I discovered I could sit in front of my laptop for hours and think. I wrote about the experience of my changing body and mind as I aged, about losing late in life love, about Covid-19 and fresh insights. The multi-layered language of poetry became my own. The result is this book.

—Madeleine May Kunin,
September 23, 2020